Polished

Steven Wesley Law

WESTBOW°
PRESS
A DIVISION OF THOMAS NELSON
& ZONDERVAN

WestBow Press books may be ordered through booksellers or by contacting:

WestBow Press
A Division of Thomas Nelson & Zondervan
1663 Liberty Drive
Bloomington, IN 47403
www.westbowpress.com
1 (866) 928-1240

Because of the dynamic nature of the Internet, any web addresses or links contained in this book may have changed since publication and may no longer be valid. The views expressed in this work are solely those of the author and do not necessarily reflect the views of the publisher, and the publisher hereby disclaims any responsibility for them.

Cover photo by Steven Law

ISBN: 978-1-4908-6826-4 (sc)
ISBN: 978-1-4908-6827-1 (e)

Library of Congress Control Number: 2015901495

Print information is available on the last page.

WestBow Press rev. date: 6/29/2015

For

My beautiful wife
Dana

Contents

Gone 1
Down Here 5
Amen! 7
Today's the Day 8
The Cottonwood with the Broken Trunk 11
Chrome 12
Dawn in Zion 14
Wild Horses 16
Thoreau's Autopsy 18
That Kind of Night 21
Another Perfect Day 24
The Shivers 27
Let's Go Camping 31
With the Tractor Idling Beside Me 34
Eighteen Kinds of Desert Water 35
How Delicious That Day Will Be 41
Coyotes, Ducks and Sunflowers 42
On the Banks of the San Juan 44
Let's Go Rafting 45
Looking Downriver from Here 51
Lessons from a River 53
Preparing the Rafts 54
A Prayer to Phyxios 56
Calling 61
Grand Canyon Trail Crew 62
Spindrift 63
Lessons from a Grand Canyon Boatman 65
Polished 66
She Runs 68

A Boatman's Toast 73
Long Division 74
The River 75
Run Together 76
An Autumn Walk 80
Dancing Around a Desert Campfire 82
A Backpacker's Rain Delay 84
It's Enough I Get to Watch 88
The Chapel of Shadows and Sunbeams 89
I Am a Poet 92
An Orangeville Apple 93
An Elegy for my Old Hiking Boots 94
A New Story 99
Heater Smell 107
Coming Home 109
A Prayer of Thanks 110
I Get Close 112

Gone

I want to find myself aboard an outbound ship
At the very beginning of a very long trip

I want to hear the riddle from the Sphinx's lips
And decipher panels in Aztec crypts
That, Baby that, is why I'm gone

I want to pursue life's elusive insights
While I'm dogsledding beneath the Northern Lights

I want to sit at the pilgrim's fire
I want to sing in the nomad's choir
That, Baby that, is why I'm gone

I want to ride a wild horse across Mongolian plains
I want to pitch my tent under African rains

I want to drown in a whirlpool of wonder
I want a riptide of awe to pull me under
That, Baby that, is why I'm gone

I want to explore the corners of the Amazon
I want to see what's beyond the Great Beyond

I want curiosity to be my guide
'Cause the horizon pulls at me
Like the moon pulls at the tide

Wait just a little longer, I'll be home soon
Just one more phase of the traveler's moon

I have a pen, a notebook and some worn-out shoes
A backpack, a blanket and a picture of you

And I've learned 20 ways to say goodbye
And a hundred ways my love proclaim
And you've learned 20 ways to ask me why
But the answer is always the same

Forty days in the desert is what I'm needin'
I want to walk those sandy trails
Till my tired feet are bleedin'

And I want to wander the Yukon's empty trails
And want to ride India's restless rails
That, Baby that, is why I'm gone

I want to find a forgotten city using antique maps
And outsmart its ancient booby-traps

I want to hear nature's delicate voices
But they're drowned out by the city's noises
That, Baby that, is why I'm gone

I want to migrate with the whales
When the zephyr fills my sails

I want to attempt the deeper contemplations
Under those Grand Canyon constellations
That, Baby that, is why I'm gone

I want to break bread with the prodigal sons
I want to taste life with the poet's tongue

I stayed put for a while.
It didn't really take but I sure tried
'Cause the horizon pulls at me
Like the moon pulls at the tide

Wait just a little longer, I'll be home soon
Just one more phase of the traveler's moon

I have a pen, a notebook and some worn-out shoes
A backpack, a blanket and a picture of you

And I've learned 20 ways to say goodbye
And you've learned 20 ways to ask me why

Wait, Baby wait, just a little longer for me
The wandering river always returns to the sea

Another campsite—and packing up at dawn
The needle settles north and now I'm gone

Down Here

Down here the afternoon virga hangs
From the clouds like pink chrysalises.
Land of narrow sky, jagged horizon.
Land of coyote, raven, lizard, bat,
Jackrabbit. Willow, tamarisk, cotton-
Wood, sagebrush. And the hidden fern
Grotto.

Where I have watched Orion make his
Slow leap from one cliff top to the other.

Up there, there have been days when my
Finer sensibilities of perception, appreciation,
Wonder were suffocating under a pavement
Of rougher qualities: aggression, competition,
Survival. But down here it's safe to unsheathe
My senses.

Down here where every wall is a ventriloquist.
I feel like these walls that surround me were
Formed to protect the precious silence and
Solitude.

If there was to be but one Spring in my
Lifetime I would make reservations to spend
It down here.

Thirsty, I have walked into your side canyons
Looking for water. And I have found it.
And I have found wine.

Amen!

The robin chirps it. The aspens clap it. The
blossoms sigh it and exhale it. The stream
laughs it. The flowers open their mouths in
hallelujahs. The lizard prostrates herself.

A Berwick's Wren foliates the air with her
enraptured singing. An American Dipper adds
its carefree, graceful garland. A Canyon Wren
adds its joyous diminuendo.

It sounds like the most sincere, most beautiful
prayer of gratitude, to be alive to enjoy
another sunny, spring day. It is all powered by
the electricity of being and feeling alive,
backlit with the truest joy.

The most I can add to this scene, this feeling
of reverence and wonder is
"Amen."

Today's the Day

I woke up to a happy, beautiful day
So I dug out my walking stick
Today's the day I called a good friend
Today's the day we called in sick

We blazed through the neighborhood
Then we skipped through the fields
And we twirled through the grass
As we hiked up the hills

Just a couple of ramblers
Gathered in carefree celebration
To rejoice in our zeal for the journey
And our love for all creation

The aspen leaves tinkled like leathery chimes
The birds sang a melodious psalm
Today we strolled along at a glacial pace
And got in tune with the forest calm

Today's the day we gathered sunshine
And got some trail dust on our shoes
Today we found inspiration
And paid our souls their IOUs

Rock to rock we hop-scotched a brook
And let a kite out to stretch her tail
We wandered wherever we wanted
Today the detour was our trail

Today we were besieged by wonders
We consulted the field guide a lot
Some rain clouds approached from the west
I think just to thicken the plot

Today's the day we spied on some deer
Today we purveyed the view
Today's the day we swam in a lake
It just seemed like a fun thing to do

Today we examined a pond for frogs
And I dared you, honey, to kiss one
"Which one should I kiss? There's so many," you said.
So I pointed to me and said, "This one."

And I laughed at your jokes
And you laughed at mine
And your vivid ghost story
Sent a jolt up my spine

Today's the day we seized the day
Today's the day we got away
Today we stopped and smelled the flowers
Now that will look good on the ol' résumé

We had a picnic amid the grass
Then rated the clouds from our backs
Today I was kissed by a beautiful girl
Now I didn't see that in the ol' almanac

Today we blew the fluff off a dandelion
And made a wish as it floated away
Our wish was simple and honest:
"May tomorrow be as good as today!"

The Cottonwood with the Broken Trunk

I do not know what brings joy to a tree.
Surely the sun upon its leaves.
Surely the taproot discovering the deep water.
And certainly it must feel great to feel the wind
Blowing through your leaves.

There was a certain tree that made me wonder
This. It stood at the intersection of Grand Gulch
And Sheiks Canyon. It had a semi-shattered
Trunk, caused by what, I do not know. I pondered
This tree and its dilemma one night while I
Camped beneath it.

Was it distressed by the wind blowing through
Its leaves knowing that the next good wind could
Topple it over? Or knowing that its days were
Numbered did it enjoy it all the more?

Though its back groaned with pain it still shook
Its leaves with what looked like delight.

Chrome

I feel like I'm slowly imploding, with
Arctic air pushing in to fill the void.
Like an inner tube full of warmth and
suppleness and this Arctic air has her
fingernail on the pin slowly bleeding
out my warmth.

This Arctic air has been vacationing in
our (normally) warmer clime and like a
generous guest our visiting Arctic air
brings with it a much appreciated gift:
snow. She continues to give us a little
more every other day. Despite all her
gifts she is gradually wearing out her
welcome. Like a neighbor who brings a
bit of sugar to sweeten your coffee but
keeps pouring in spoonful after spoon-
ful until the coffee is ruined.

I draw my scarf around my face so only
an eye-slit remains. It smells like I'm
walking through an orchard of iron shav-
ings just blooming.

Just off the trail in front of me snow
tumbles off a pine bough and breaks up
into thousands of snow crystals which
spin to the ground in undulating drapes,
rippling like a flag. It moves through the
air like a chrome version of the northern
lights, at first billowing out into a sail, then
crenellating into a sequined curtain.
Beautiful!

I want to see it again so I stop and make a
snowball to throw at another snow-laden
branch. I stand so the target tree is be-
tween me and the sun to optimize the
twinkle effect. The snow is so dry that
packing a snowball is like doing that trick
with cornstarch. I believe it's called
Ooblech (Ooblech: eight tablespoons corn-
starch, four tablespoons water, mix together).
As soon as I stop compressing the snowball
it turns to powder and pours through my
fingers. I try it again. This time humidifying
the dry snowball with my breath.

I take aim at a snow-laden branch. Pfooph!
A silver cloud of diamond spores twinkles to
the ground. A galaxy is born. I do it over and
over again just to watch the snow crystals
which glitter like lightning chaff, mists of
atomized sequins, a mirror disintegrating into
pollen.

Dawn in Zion

Even though I pass less than a horseshoe's pitch
away from her, she looks at me with the unworried
assurance that comes from having lived her life
within the safety of a national park. Two fawns
curl into her warmth, still sleeping.

On the trail towards Angel's Landing. The sun's not
yet up, but it's still light enough to see without a
flashlight. It's that rare time of day when birds and
bats share the same airspace, pursuing insects.
Violet green swallows zip overhead, "sshhppt"
like cruise missiles. The bats dart about more
acrobatically, bouncing through the air like
marionettes on elastic bands.

Angel's Landing, island in the sky. A fin of rock
jutting out from Cathedral Mountain like a thumb
from a hand, offering a 360 degree view of the
interior of the park. I reach the top of Angel's Landing
shortly after the sun comes up.

Jigsawed canyon walls emerge from the Narrows
In parallel zigzags of wedges and Vs,
like a zipper unzipped. I watch the
chipmunks play and the hawks soar
below me.

I just sit and watch the shadows cast from the cliff walls on the east end of the canyon scroll down the cliff faces on the west end of the canyon, then recede across the canyon floor like water left from an outgoing tide.

Wild Horses

The armada of blue-shadowed cauliflower clouds is too
weak a shield to protect me from the afternoon's heat. I
take shelter in the twisted shade of a squatty juniper on
a mesa overlooking the mouth of a canyon.

The temperature isn't the only thing climbing. The air fills
with a phantom uneasiness, an expectant silence. Like the
smell of ozone before a lightning strike, or the weight of
unseen eyes on the back of your head.

I'm not the only one who feels it.

I am boredly dividing my attention between picking at a
lichen scab growing on a nearby rock and watching a
column of ants climb the juniper tree under which I'm
sitting. Suddenly, every ant in the column of ants, as if on
signal from their sergeant, stops in its tracks. After pausing

For two or three seconds they, once again in unison,
commence their upward march. Sparrows suddenly unbird
a neighboring juniper and locusts erupt from the sagebrush
on ratchety wings with a sound like sticks being stroked over
washboards.

The phantom apprehension slowly adds flesh to itself.
I can feel their approach a full minute before I hear them.
A deep resonation curdling through the earth.
I am sitting cross-legged on an outspread poncho.
It's as if I'm sitting on the end of a long table
and someone at its far end is tapping their fingers on its
surface.

I stand up.
The vibrations get stronger,
until I feel them at the base of my spine, then in my kidneys.
About the time I can hear them I feel the earth's vibrations
in my chest, rumbling through my heart like iambic spurts
of adrenaline

The force of 320 unshod hooves
funneling down the canyon.

Thoreau's Autopsy

When the great poet Henry Thoreau passed on
I wonder what they would have found
(If they had performed an autopsy)
In the sack that contained his heart.

Would they have found a heart sprouting with
Long antennae or delicate tendrils?
That delicately reached into the places that
Others had ignored?
Antennae that reached into the pilot snake's lair

Under the mussel's shell, into the mockingbird's
Nest, that caressed the tassels on the corn, gently
Searched the apple blossom, ruffled the bee's
Velvet back, softly pried into the peach pit.

Antennae that twined with the antennae of
Butterflies and the ivy's succulent tendrils, held
The crystals of the snowflake. Tendrils that had
Climbed the black oak like a tingle up the spine,

Causing the branches and leaves to shiver.
Antennae that brought back messages to be de-
Coded, decrypted by that wonderful, feeling heart.
Feelers that had transferred messages from

The pitch pines, the zephyr, the field mouse, the
Cricket, the Indian summer. Antennae that brought
Back the lightning and the flame. Antennae that
Plugged into the base of our spines to share with us

The shivers of rapture.
Or would they have looked more like the snail's
Gelatinous feelers? Carefully, cautiously
Feeling out the way ahead, softly touching,

Sometimes flinching back with a wince.
Or would they have found a tiny *malleus* and *stapes,*
Hammer and stirrup? Much like the one found
In the ear, but this one attuned to the vibration and

Language of the universe. Or would they have
Found a prism that separates the light of under-
Standing into decipherable bars of
Eureka!

Certainly they would have discovered there a
Heart very well exercised, well used. And it would
Seem, to me, at least, that his body must have
Begged to be put into the ground.

There to dissolve into life
For his trees, the fox, the blue jays. Now to peer at
The world through the owl's nocturnal eyes, the high
Vantage of the leaves

The den of the mole, riding on the back of a yellow
Butterfly, or in the raindrop, the song of a
Meadowlark, the oak's meditation, the spring
Meadow's rapture.

And where, I now, a fellow poet, and lover of this
World, must wonder, where is that great soul now?
Back among his friends, his colleagues, his confidants,
The blossom, the raven, the velvet fungus, the willow?

Or, perhaps reincarnated as Mary Oliver.

That Kind of Night

It's that kind of night. When you light a
scented candle and your kitchen is translated
into a rainforest. It's the kind of night when
you spread six month's worth of *National*

Geographics on the table and read them all
cover to cover. It's the kind of night when
you make yourself some tea and wish for a
harmonica and a dog to keep you company.

A warm breeze catches in the curtains and
poofs them out like a smock over a pregnant
woman's belly. The heat is a good heat for
this kind of night. A slow, contemplative

Heat that make the stories you read in your
National Geographics seem more poignant,
more meaningful than perhaps they really
are. It's the kind of night that awakens old

Dreams, old plans. Your old attitude. Your
old optimism. You remember your old way
of thinking. You remember the possibilities.
And that's the night you decide that it's time

To go. It is something that you cannot put
off anymore. It is not an errand. It is just a
growing within you. Some kind of instinct.
Like the flower blooms for no other reason

Than that it's time to bloom. Like the
caterpillar weaving its cocoon knows not
why. You have been feeling this swelling,
this growing within yourself. Your eye is ever

More drawn to the horizon. You cannot stop
it any more than the snake can prevent
growing out of his old skin. You can't ignore
it anymore. You just leave. You know it's

Safer, more comfortable, in your familiar
little pond, but still you go. Like the salmon
swimming upstream you may not understand
why you're going until you reach the end of

The journey. The same voice that calls the
salmon upstream, the same voice that calls the
geese south for the winter is now calling to
you. How long can you ignore hearing your

Name being called before you set out to see who is calling it? You go to the car and check the gas gauge. What yesterday you saw as half empty, you now see as half full.

Another Perfect Day

It wasn't the Yellowstone River gleaming green
as an edge of thick glass. It wasn't the sky that
was clear for the first time in weeks.
It wasn't that this was the first day all winter that

We could feel the sun regaining its strength.
It wasn't the bison across the river grazing
on the trampled grass. It wasn't the trees
tilted over the water at the angle of arrows

Shot from great distances. Nor the long, golden
pockets of grass swept like flames before a wind.
It wasn't these things that made it a perfect day.
These things merely made it a beautiful day.

It wasn't the trail, high on the mountainside, that
was new and unexplored. It wasn't the trail
preaching freedom to our feet.
This only made it an adventurous day.

You found mountain lion tracks in the dried mud,
and knelt down and held your hand over them to
compare size, then looked up and scanned the
cliffs. She might still be nearby! That inquisitive,

Childlike look in your eyes as you hopefully looked
(beautiful!)
This added wonder and discovery to our day.
But not even this made it a perfect day.

It was sitting with you on the black rocks,
smoothed by the river. It was leaning back
against you, tucked in the warm V of your legs,
your fingers locked in mine across my belly.

It was rising on your inhalations and falling with
your exhalations like a raft on the swells of a gentle
ocean. It wasn't the trout quietly sipping
mayflies off the water's surface. It wasn't

Watching the flat water turning over, like soil
behind a plow, as it entered the narrow
part of the stream. It was having you with me as
we explored the new trail, as we felt the born-

Again sun on our cheeks and arms. It was my fingers
buried in your sun-warmed hair, my
fingertips caressing your sun-rouged cheeks,
your eyes sparkling like the sun on the Gallatin.

Beauty, adventure, wonder, exploration,
meditation, discovery, joy, enlightenment and
love, (that rare, crimson strand) are the
threads with which I wish to weave my life.

How fortunate that I was allowed to weave a
part of my life with a part of yours. Even if only
for one glorious, perfect day. For one
glorious, perfect winter.

The Shivers

I want to capture this day and put it on display
Forever encased in one of those little souvenir
Snow globes. And every once in a while take
It down off the shelf and look in on it.

Look down onto the
Little scene just now unfolding
And give the globe a little shake . . .
To get the snow falling again.

I see again the soft profiles of the hills,
Swept like the curve between your hip and
Shoulder. The snow-covered pines look like
Brides in hoop skirts. Imagine

A pine forest growing atop a cloud
And you've got the picture.
Look closer into the globe and you will see a
Solitary man steadily walking north through the

Snow. Like walking through an endless bead curtain,
He thinks to himself. Snowshoes squeaking, geysers of
Labored breath dissipate slowly in the still air, scarf
Wrapped around his ears, tied under his chin.

Stalactites of frost hang from his mustache and
Beard. Steep mountains border him on the east and west.
He steps out from a lane in the pines and climbs the last
Few steps up onto the crest of the narrow mountain pass

And contemplates the vista before him while he rests.
Western sky the color of steel dust.
Snowflakes fall like silver-blue asterisks. The mountains in
The distance slowly diminish behind the screen of falling

Snow as if on a rheostat. Disorienting. He can't tell, for sure,
Which direction he's going. No sun. Low visibility.
Even while he watches the mountains fade to
Gray, to translucent shadows, then disappear.

Unreliable as a mirage.
He checks the compass that hangs from his neck. A map
Hibernates in his backpack. He knows the way.
A platoon of bison patrols the snowfield on his left.

Some raise their long, patriarchal faces, regard him with
The patience of the weary. He regards them with the wonder
Of a child. He walks around them slowly, watching them (bursting!),

Not wanting to disturb their feeding. Step, step, pause.
Step, step, pause. Like escorting a bride down the aisle.
Last Autumn he gave his heart the reins and it led him here.
Like a witching stick shivers when it finds water, his heart now

Shivers here in Yellowstone, testifying that it has divined him a
New home. And his neck hairs stand erect to confirm it. He
Believes that this same heart can now lead him out of this
    blizzard
Back to a heart that worries for him. Back to arms that miss him.

A solitary man steadily walking through the snow, snowshoes
Squeaking, geysers of labored breath dissipate slowly in the
    still air,

Scarf wrapped around his ears, tied under his chin. Stalactites of
    frost
Hang from his mustache and beard. His heart shivers.

He is anything but numb.

Let's Go Camping

The woods are full of wonders
Let's go try a few on for size
Lift up a rock and take a peek under
And look a bug right in its eyes

Or you can skip a stone across the lake
And ponder the ripples that you make

You can climb a mountain to its peak
And feel the sunshine kiss your cheek

When you hear a songbird, join in its song
And when you find a stream, why, wade along

Cast your voice into a canyon
It will soon come bouncing back
It only takes a couple shouts
Before you get the knack

You can float down a river in a big canoe
And try to catch a fish or two

Feel the gentle wind blow through your hair
And fill your lungs with that sweet pine air

A magnifying glass is good to include
For times when you're in a woods-snooping mood

You'll make discoveries of every kind
And you can make a scrapbook of the cool things you find

Don't despair if you see lightning flash
Rain can be lots of fun
There are frogs to catch and puddles to splash
Plus there's a rainbow when it's done

Camping in the spring is really quite awesome
When the fields are abloom and the trees are in blossom

In the summer walk through a meadow of flowers
And later that night we'll watch a meteor shower

In the autumn jump in a big leaf pile
And take some pictures every once in a while

In the winter walk through the falling snow
And then sit by the fire and drink cocoa

The forest is so beautiful
What you see may first astound you

Let your mother guide you down the trail
And pause now and then to look around you

Watching the sunset's a fun thing to do
(This is good advice for grown-ups too)

To put the *great* back in the great outdoors
Just make yourself a couple s'mores

That great campfire smell will get trapped in your clothes
While you bask in tall tales round the campfire's glow

And have your dad point out Venus and Mars
While you're in your sleeping bag under the stars

Camp and explore as much as you can
When you grow up you'll be glad you did
And the most important thing of all:
Don't forget to be a kid!

With the Tractor Idling Beside Me

I have done it so many times. In my backyard, in mountain meadows, on southern Utah slickrock. Lying on my back, looking up at the sky, watching the clouds pass. As if they're below me. The trick is to lie with your head in the direction the wind is blowing from. Pretend that the sky is the ocean. Pretend you're flying high above the clouds. Let the clouds drifting by give the illusion that you're moving. That you're flying!

One time in British Columbia little imagination was needed. I gave the sea kayak four quick backward strokes and leaned back. Mist lying close to the water lent the feeling that I was flying through the clouds. And the stars became a city far below me. During a cozy Yellowstone snowstorm I actually felt myself falling as the snow floated towards me. Up here I'm free. Up here I can go wherever I want. It's a skill I perfected lying in the wheat, oat and hayfields growing up on my father's farm. With the tractor idling beside me.

Eighteen Kinds of Desert Water

Frog Broth
A pothole of old rainwater Swimming with tadpoles water
Beetles water skeeters Visited by wasps deer hummingbirds
An acquired taste
Of salamanders and frogs simmered in lukewarm water
With additive of dissolved iodine if you have it

The Hermit's Bathwater
From a ways back it looks like coffee
Clotted with duff and detritus
But push the detritus aside Dip in your canteen
You'll find it's actually quite clear
And tastes pretty good

Fern Spring
The explorer upon returning home after a long journey
When first looking upon his front door
Knowing the woman he
Loves waits behind it is filled with a certain feeling
He will try to convey to her later
Drinking from the fern spring tastes something like that
But diluted

Narcissus's Crucible
Cloudy and chunky
Like trying to swallow a hendecasyllable
Or German phrase
The water is stirred up as if the prison ward floundered in it
During a mass baptism
The water still tastes like sin

Running Stream
There are two things that fill a desert explorer's
Heart with joy that goes deep as the mesquite's taproot
One of them is a stream of fresh clear water

Cuspidor Soup
Smells like moldy hay And leper squeezins
Viscous as bird's nest soup Like drinking a quid of
Masticated tobacco
Tastes great after being lost for 36 hours

Afterbirth Tea
The surface of the water has a placental covering of dust
Dead beetles leaves
With your hand push this aside Then below that
Push aside the phlegmy green dreadlocks of moss and

Plunge in your cup Be prepared to chew a little
Will effectively wash down the Ibuprofen

Map of the Universe
Crawl from your night tent Kneel at the edge of the pool
Lean forth to drink Surface shimmering with bioluminescent
Insects You think At first Oh!
Those are mirrored stars! Acknowledge the chill of realization
It gives you
Drink
Contemplate your place

Asbestos Tea
A stale pothole surrounded by cracked mud
Foggy as a December windshield
A chemical composition undoubtedly closer to raw sewage
Than it is to rainwater
Tastes like smog
Leaves your throat feeling itchy

Yuppies' Bathwater
It's the only water for eight miles around
And its surface is coated with a film of sunscreen
Washed off the clueless weekend warriors who dipped in to
Cool off
If desire for revenge had a taste I believe it would taste like this

Fresh Rainwater in a Pothole
Dissolves cotton
A feeling like euphoria gorging itself on joy
To drink it
Rejuvenates the blood that will fuel today's beautiful journey
Deeper into the canyon
But this pothole of fresh rainwater lies like a sacred offering
Beneath a pictograph gallery of
Triangular faces and handprints
A tribute to ancient ancestors
I dare not drink of it

The Devil's Bloody Mary
Half coagulated with suspended sand particles
Thick as martyr's blood
Like drinking pumice
Better if strained through a bandanna

The Flowing River
Wade in Swim Cool your weary body
Most often being plied by cheerful boatmen
Who will inquire of your health and home
And always offer you food and drink

The Bait and Switch
A pothole filled with clear cool sweet water
But may contain
Giardia or
Tincture of arsenic
Like the razor blade hiding in the apple

Tadpole Chowder
Found in swampy canyon bottom Or on sunbaked cliff top
A rapidly drying August pothole
More tadpoles than water A glutinous gray stew
Fetid Rancid Sour More mucous than water
You know from sad experience its
Best not to pass by if resources allow

Prospector's Sluicebox
After the flashflood
Your only choice

The Green Mask
Its surface upholstered with a green suede mask
Of moss Which you pull aside to fill your canteen
Thrum-like green tentacles hang from its bottom side
Water beetles dart for deeper water like cockroaches
Surprised by the light
But it is well-oxygenated Tastes delicious

Deathbed Repentance
Your bottles are empty You are thirsty
And you do not know where the next water will be found
Nor how far away it may be
And then there it is!
A pothole of water
Clear or cloudy Fresh or briny Sweet or brackish
Doesn't matter
Contains alchemical properties that transforms the lead
Weight of worry into
Golden relief!

How Delicious That Day Will Be

How delicious that day will be
When I will take the new book from my favorite
Author—it waits on the bookshelf even now—and
Sit under my favorite tree on the soft new grass
Of spring, in the soft new warmth of spring.

In a place where pine trees silhouetted atop banisters
Of cliff wall look like passengers riding an escalator.

Such a day can't help but contain some magic
Sprouting up through the damp soil, with the marigold
And rock daisies, their tiny green fists pushing triumphantly
From the damp soil.

In a place bounded on all sides with orange and vermilion
Cliff walls that catch and translate the expressions and
Moods of the sunlight.

How chilly the breeze will be on my skin that day. How
Chilly the breeze will feel on the moist petals of the
Newborn flowers. I'll meet you there daisies and marigolds
On the other side of this frost, snow and these long nights.

In the place with the dunes, the willows, the loneliness,
The lightning-felled Cottonwood. Where the two rivers join.
Where the silence and crickets alternate shifts.

With a long, sandy trail leading to it.

Coyotes, Ducks and Sunflowers

I used to walk through a field
That was home to long grass and sunflowers
Coyotes, rabbits and skunks
Used to hide there.
Flowers used to stand there and shine.
Now it's filled with houses.

I used to walk through an orchard
That was home to apple and apricot trees
Robins, jays and finches
Held forums in the heavy boughs.
One day a bulldozer came.
Now it's filled with houses.

I used to walk past a lake
That was home to ducks, wrens and otters.
Hawks, ospreys and eagles
Patrolled the thermals above.
It was surrounded by cattails, reeds and muddy banks.
Now the lake is covered with boats, the banks covered with
Houses.

I used to walk to a point that overlooked the green valley
That was home to aspens, cottonwoods and deer.

Turkeys, grouse and pheasants
Used to forage in the undergrowth.
A clear stream ran through it.
Now it's filled with smog and beige houses.

People are fine, and people need homes.
But coyotes, ducks and sunflowers do too.

On the Banks of the San Juan

Sitting with a knife, whittling driftwood
Looking out across the river
Watching the imbricating waves
Pushing on to the beach

Beyond, the cliff walls are
Bathed in pilsner-colored light
That feels syrupy and warm on my clammy skin

Watching the river
That old and favorite boatman past time
That tonight the
Moonlight shall transform into rippling mercury

It is easy to understand why the Navajos
Once believed the earth was sung
Into existence

The river still sings an alluring song
That I have heard this week while traveling its length
The river still sways, and dances to the song she sings

I hear her, I watch her. I want to take her in my arms and dance
With her
I can't say I know the steps
But I sure do like the rhythm

Let's Go Rafting

The river is running, the rapids are roaring
Adventure waits for us down below!
The sun is shining, the canyon is calling
Air up the boats, grab your oars, let's go!

Rowing and fishing will make up our labors
Ravens and wrens will be our noisiest neighbors

Huge waves will wash over us again and again
But they won't be enough to wash off our grins

And we'll feel our priorities slowly shifting
After twelve happy days of rowing and drifting

And for a stretch, at least, we'll do like Siddhartha
We won't plan, we won't row, we won't steer
We'll practice the Tao of the Muddy River
We'll slow down till things settle and grow clear

A river's one of those wonderful places
It's a beautiful, tree-lined, linear oasis

Now, hold tight! the first rapid draws closer
And it's an enormous, playful roller-coaster

Just try to forget that this rapid scares ya!
But c'mon, go big, drop the hole, I dare ya!

C'mon grab your paddle, get back in the saddle
It's time to enter the fray
When the rapids roar, hold tight to your oars
Let's get our first blast of spray

Monster waves crash on your side, tsunamis break on my side
Keep an eye on the girl in the ducky!
Square up and *Bam!* be ready to highside
We might make it through if we're lucky

Colossal waves pound us, fore and aft
Duck down, brace and be brave
If we live we'll practice the Tao of the Raft
When euphoria washes o'er us in waves

Yup, there's something magical about river spray
You see, rapids can wash your troubles away

But, a river trip's not an adventurous race
Some say the best parts are the long peaceful stretches
We'll let the flow of the river dictate our pace
We'll go just slow enough for transcendence to catch us

We'll ship the oars and drift
And let the raft spin
And watch the light change on the cliffs
Like chameleon skin

We'll contemplate the river and its myriad swirls
We'll think about the wave and the way that it curls

The river will give us sweet memories
She'll show us her splendor as she slowly unscrolls
And she'll share with us her mysteries
Yup, that's just how the river rolls

Our river guide will point out the things around us
And his tall tales and lies will nearly drown us

From time to time we'll leave the river corridor
And go see what lies beyond the shore
Side canyons offer so much to explore
We'll find wildlife, paradise and possibly more

We may find an ancient ruin along a sacred trail
We may find a plunge pool below a waterfall's veil

Perhaps we'll find a fern grotto or a flowery glade
The perfect place to nap or read a book in the shade

Maybe we'll find some pictographs or petroglyphs
Or look down at our rafts from the top of the cliffs

And then it's back to the boats to make some miles
You and me and the rest of these crazy aqua-philes

All day we've had those oars in our hands
But now it's time to bury our toes in the sand
This river life's even better than we had planned
Yup, life's pretty good when your toes are tanned

This is a good time to practice the River Effect
When we, like the river, slow down and reflect

Forget your cell phone, your laptop and all those things
And connect with the peace that disconnection brings

We'll cut the potatoes and fillet the fishes
Then we'll fry 'em up, man, that's delicious!

For an unbeatable dose of backcountry lovin'
We'll eat peach cobbler from an old Dutch oven

We'll build a campfire and tell some stories
Recounting the close calls and all the day's glories
We'll tell of stunning sights, water fights, and rapids roaring
Each tale as beautiful as a fleet of dories

And we'll bang the buckets and strum the guitars
We'll sing for the bats, the spiders and stars

We'll drift off to sleep to the sound of crickets
Or to a silence most profound
Or it may be the white noise of a rapid
Ah! the river makes a joyful sound

And indeed our priorities have shifted
During these sweet days that we've pondered and drifted

It's alright. It's cool. It's just as well
That we leave here under the river's spell

Now snug in our sleeping bags we'll fall asleep
Safe inside our canyon deep

It takes just about a week
To achieve the Mirror Principle
Which is, when you look in the river long enough
Your true self becomes visible

Yes! A river is a wonderful thing
Yes! A river is a magical being

It can turn 18 feet of rubber into a magic carpet
So grab your friends, grab the oars, let's get this adventure
    started!

Looking Downriver from Here

The pontoons are aired up and lashed on
And now there is time to catch my breath and look around.
I eat an apple in the back of the raft and watch AZRA
Rig their fleet. Oars, straps, coolers and 20 mils scattered
Across the gravel river bank.

It will be good to be downriver again.
Where Navajo tapestry adorns the cliff walls
Like Rorshaach faces.

Boatmen from three commercial companies and
Two private trips wander the gravel beach. We wear sandals,
Faded hats, holey t-shirts. Some wear pliers on their belts.

At the far end of the beach a private trip rigs their rafts.
Offloading ammo cans, coolers and produce from
The back of a truck. Five kayaks—two yellow, three red— sit
With their tails in the river, their noses on the beach.

Yes, it's good to be going downriver again.
Where the bighorns gather
Where the ravens always watch
Where the Owl Eyes never close.

Powell stood here. Georgie stood here. Loper
Stood here. The Kolbs, the Sandersons, the Poulsons
Have stood right here on this same gravel bank and rigged their
Boats, embellished their stories, perfected their lies. I wonder,
Did a feather of exhilaration tickle their adrenal glands, as it
Does mine, when they shoved their boats off the bank?

There is a feeling I get every time I'm here that I've been trying
To define. What is it? Now, halfway through my second season I
Think I've at last defined it:
I feel that I'm a seed, perhaps, and
A determined finger is pushing me into fertile soil.

As day passes into darkness swampers and boatmen gather
Together on an AZRA boat and blow the devil from the bottle.
The runs through Horn Creek, Hance and Lava Falls are never
So bold, so brave as when told here in this liar's cathedral.

I eat my apple.
I look downriver.
I wonder where this river will take me.

Lessons from a River

Run wild
Disappear around a bend
Slow down and reflect
Be free
Meander when needed
Push forward
Slow down until things settle and grow clear
She will tell you her greatest secrets only when you
    reach her mouth

Preparing the Rafts

Today the heat radiates through thin warehouse
walls that ring with rowdy industry. But soon the
heat I feel will radiate off silent cliff walls.

Today the flash and flare I see comes from the
artificial spark of Jimmy Cat's welding torch
but soon I'll be seeing the flicker and pop of
lightning from our camp at Nankoweap.

Soon I'll be seeing the Little Colorado River's
verdigrised waters running through brown-rock
canyons, not so different than this raft paint that
today runs down my tan leg.

Anticipation and excitement inflate inside me.
And they rub and chafe against each other like
our rafts tied at Havasu, as they tug and strain
against the ropes, they too, eager to be back on
the river.

Soon I'll be standing on the beach at Schist
listening to the thunder rolling through the
canyon. But today the only thunder I hear is that

of the pontoons dragging across the gravel at
Lee's Ferry.

Yes, soon I'll be watching the sun rise on the
cliff walls from lower Saddle, the same color as
these faded lifejackets I now sort through on
the warehouse floor.

A Prayer to Phyxios

My dreams were destroyed, and my mind was charred
My screams were deployed, and my heart was scarred

Defeated and ruined I walked down the street
Through shimmering waves that rose up from the heat
That melted my spirit and blistered my feet
But on I marched to its terrible automaton beat

Where money muffles the music with how loudly it talks
And the t.v. preaches fear to its horrified flocks
And greed spreads and destroys with its terrible pox
Killing even that which remained in Pandora's Box

I was trapped in Progress's pointless odyssey
Producing to produce was our greatest commodity
Facebook and texts were our brand of camaraderie
My loathing for it all was considered an oddity

Wisdom is needed but can hardly be found
Though poets and prophets in abundance abound
But their words have been cut and further dumbed down
Just keep moving forward and keep your eyes on the ground

Just step into line and remember your place
Don't go too fast nor slow down the pace
Keep your eye on the carrot we're all here to chase
And keep a look of contentment on your botoxed face

If you wanna buy the junk they advertise
Just show up in your suit and your xeroxed ties
When you look in the mirror don't look in your eyes
Now trade it all in for the next biggest size

And return to the valley of Barbie doll wives
And your hollow molded plastic lives
Back to your neighborhood of cookie-cut houses
Just repeat and repeat till the last check bounces

How can I hit my stride?
Where the engines idle and the iPods shuffle
And what is the use of singing?
Where industry deafens and the masses muffle

I need to escape the sterility of your unisex bathrooms
And the mind-numbing musings of your meaningless
    chatrooms

I don't want your sitcom opinions at your vapid water coolers
And I'm done rubbing shoulders with the do goodie carpoolers

My life as hollow as the pipes they smoked
And the ignorance as dense as the exhaust that I choked

My longing for adventure was strictly forbidden
It was best just to keep it locked up or hidden

This is not the life I had planned for myself
Just how did my dreams end up on the shelf?

Through what wicked chance did I end up here?
Doing petty things under virtue's veneer
Well, I can't do it for another year
What kind of escape can I engineer?

No! This was not the life for me!!!
I was not the person I was meant to be
I was meant to roar, I was meant to run free
I was meant to live more daringly

I wanted a life filled with happy surprises
I wanted to witness ten thousand happy sunrises

I wanted to stand where Thoreau once stood
I wanted to walk or maybe run through the woods

I wanted a place where I could still be a man
I wanted a place to finish this quest I began

It only hurt when I thought of the wonders I missed
And it ground in my soul like an industrial fist

"I'm gonna find that place, and I'm leaving right now to do it!"
And I left right then and there to prove it

And now the wind is blowing, and camp's five miles away
The exact same conditions as yesterday

From the mouths of the peeps the questions are spilling
And my poor, cracked hands have lost all feeling
Yeah, sure I'm tired but my soul is willing
The problem is, my back is killing

But, I once broke my back doing something I hated
That almost left me broken, and most certainly jaded

Now I break my back doing something I love
And, believe me, that makes all the difference, bud

Now I proudly give it all I can give her
Oh heavens it's good to be back on the river

I once pushed through the hordes on the sidewalks
Where street corner cameras watched us like hawks
But down here I've discovered a strange paradox
The hawks all but ignore us from their perch on the rocks

I once stood in line for the eight dollar buffet
Now I eat from awe's cornucopia every day

The sun, which sees all, looked upon me with disgrace
He called forth the clouds to hide the shame on his face

But now I row along under the bluest of skies
On a day so bright it kind of hurts my eyes

And my candle which once burned at both ends
Now into the wax of peace it descends

Now I row my boat and I toss my pliers
And I cook my meals over propane fires

Yes, I was rescued by this beautiful river
I'll forever be grateful is the promise I give Her

My life wants beauty, adventure, poetry and exploration
Wonder, joy, enlightenment, discovery and meditation

I found *all* of those things on this river I roam
And that is why I call the Grand Canyon my home

Calling

a button lying in a box amongst other
buttons looks natural, quite comfortable
looks like it belongs

but what the button really wants is
to be
sewn to the shirt and pushed through
the buttonhole

Grand Canyon Trail Crew

The day's work lies behind me
A crescent moon rises before me

Busy swallows dart about me
A blessed peace grows within me

A contented weariness weighs on me
A bountiful sigh lifts off me

A soft wind blows against me
Some good friends wait for me

A hot plate will be passed to me
A prayer of thanks will emerge from me

A rocky trail turns beneath me
The first stars appear above me

Spindrift

We drove into the setting sun, toward the
Mauve stain spilling down the western sky
Like wine down a boatman's lifejacket
And on into the dusk.

As darkness overtook us we lashed our two
Rafts together, killed the motors, lifted them from
The rocks in the river. Silence rushed into the vacuum.

We drifted down the dark river
The four guides met in the back of the boats, chatted,
Shared a dinner of bread and cold meat.
It was a warm and humid night.
Like lover's breath

The rafts brushed or bumped into the cliff walls,
Not a lot, just every so often, their
Rubber bodies bouncing harmlessly away
The brush and bump started us spinning.

I moved to a pile of sleeping pads and dry bags and laid
Down. Listened to the whisper of the river
Like parents talking low in the other room
And gazed at the stars spinning slowly above

The Milky Way, which looked like a long, white beach
Slowly spinning as I drifted off to sleep

Morning approached
Still
Drifting
Down the river

From inside my sleeping bag I watched the stars disappear
And watched the cliff walls turn blue
To purple, to pink

Aries was one of the last constellations to rise that
Morning. And part of Taurus—Pleiades and Aldebaran—
Rose above the horizon before dissolving in the light
Of dawn

And behind Taurus was Orion
Still buried
15 degrees below the horizon

Like me, he's there but can't be seen
Like me, he will re-appear in late September

Lessons from a Grand Canyon Boatman

Don't be afraid to jump in
Look ahead
Let yourself be moved
Try a new angle
Keep yourself centered
Pull your own weight
You can't control the river,
    the current, the rapid or the
    waves; but you control the
    oars that control the raft
Go big
Rock the boat every once in a while
Return to the source
Don't rush the trip

Polished

As broken glass after a million waves
have crashed against the beach
Or the ship's hull, pushed over 10,000 horizons
by 10,000 winds

As the steps of the monastery long traveled
by eight centuries of monks
Or this old bar top buffed by six generations
of heavy, workman's elbows

As polished as the log over the manger
where 20 generations of pack mules
Rubbed their hungry necks
Or the cliff walls brushed by 40 millenia of wind

As polished as the widow's walk
Where the beautiful wife anxiously watches
the storm-dark sea

Even jagged granite is smoothed by the river's
constant flowing

Be not as the glacier's grinding weight, which, as it leaves
only shatters, only crushes. The secret is be gentle
yet unceasing

As polished as the handle of my walking staff after
40 days in the desert
Or the handles of my oars after eight seasons
on the river

Or the speech I deliver; why I must, once again, be going

She Runs

She was born in the Rocky Mountain's shadow
On the western slope of Colorado
It was a lost man's road that led me to her

She lifts me up, then she pulls me under
She suspends me in her world of wonder
No love, my love, has ever been truer

I hear her freedom song calling to me
I feel her current surging through me
I feel her restlessness pulsing through my blood

I want to stroke her beautiful, gleaming skin
I want to soak in her wisdom, I want to drink her in
But I have only this small vessel with which to catch the flood

And she runs and she runs and she runs
And she calls: Run with me
She calls: run with me
She calls: run with me . . .
And I go

But she's trapped inside walls of her own making
And she's used up from all the taking
But she's my goddess, my queen, my Magdalene

She's both my harbor and my tempest
She's both my goddess and my temptress
She's the most beautiful siren I've ever seen

She's both my book and my favorite passage
She's both my world and my trusted atlas
She's my fortress and my freedom

She's the author of my magic days
She made the temple where I come to pray
She gives me courage, confidence when I most need 'em

And I'll run with her, while I'm still foolish
Brave and strong
May the journey be ever wild
May the journey be ever long

And she runs, and she runs, and she runs
Like a train running off a cliff
And she carries me with her
To the depths of her abyss

And she runs and she runs and she runs
And she calls: Run with me
She calls: run with me
She calls: run with me . . .
And I go

She's down and she's dirty and full of grit
She's my doorway to the infinite
And she runs smooth as whiskey down the tongue

I want to run, though my prospects may be slim
I don't know if I'll go the distance
I don't know if I'll sink or swim
I don't know if I'm ready but
I'm ready to take the plunge

I can taste the universe when I bring her to my lips
But when I pull her in through my fingers she slips
I better taste her sweetness after I've been gone

She haunts me every time I leave her
She's like the nightmare inside the fever
Her path is the path where I most belong

And she runs and she runs and she runs
And she calls: Run with me
She calls: run with me
She calls: run with me . . .
And I go

And yes, she will fall repeatedly
But she'll not be stopped so easily
She'll bring me with her on her electric tide

She once ran wild and free, untouched by man
But now she's trapped and dirty, and 15 times dammed
But she'll die before she's Pacified

Sometimes she's as calm as a hero's hand
Sometimes she's as restless as Sahara sand
But I say run baby run, I'll follow wherever you wend

And one day my river will carry me home
And that's where you'll find me, lost and alone
When this gorgeous season at last comes to an end

And I'll run with her, while I'm still young and strong
May the journey be a wild one, may the journey be long

And she runs, and she runs, and she runs
Like a train running off a cliff
And she carries me with her
To the depths of her abyss

And she runs and she runs and she runs
And she calls: Run with me
She calls: run with me
She calls: run with me . . .
And I go

A Boatman's Toast

May our runs be slick
May the booty be sick
May we have no hits
May we have no flips
And if we must drown
May we drown in tips

Long Division

You're far away, 'midst stone and glass towers
In a beautiful city by the bay
I'm here among the cliffs and the flowers
On another gorgeous Grand Canyon day

I miss the strength your assuring kiss imparts
I miss your calming voice and gentle way
Your touch that gives courage to a fearful heart
I could really use some of that today

But, now your absence feels like an eternity
After six long months of being gone
We are like ten divided by three
It's left a fraction that goes on and on

With long division comes much subtraction
And nothing can split like the river rives
A rift that grows wider with the season's protraction
It seems the only thing adding up are the negatives

But we've done the math, and we have the proof
We'll have a remainder when this problem is through

The River

Rive (riv), verb 1. To tear or rend apart. 2. To separate

It can cut through all that is solid
It can cut through all that's uplifting
Pledges, oaths, even true love
As easily as Coconino sandstone.

It's not because it's strong, though it is strong.
It's not because it's swift, though it is swift, but
Because it never stops.

After a season you'll see some wear
But it's bridgeable
But season after season

The constant friction becomes more noticeable
And eventually exposes the
Rough layers, hidden faces, the hearts of stone
And every fault.

Run Together

I used to row the big rapids
Through youthful days I thought would last forever
Down where the Green, the San Juan
And the Colorado run together

It's a strange deal, it feels kind of surreal
When your endless summer finally comes to an end
But alas, a river isn't something you can keep
The best you can do is drink real deep

And I used to run with the best of 'em
Nate and Richard, Okie and Jack
Al and Wilbur, Clanky and Zach

We rowed through April gales, blowing five foot swells
And every kind of nasty weather
But we also had beautiful days of sunshine
We were a tight crew, that ran together

I know now that it was wrong
But I didn't know I'd be gone so long

I only went to see what I could find
But that meant leaving a few things behind

And now the wind in the willows sounds like her sigh
On the day I packed up and said goodbye

Then a letter arrived at Phantom Ranch
That said, "I don't know how much longer I can wait."
And I ran and I ran and I ran to get her
But I got there too late

She was skinny and small, but she stood tall
And she let her silence say it all

And the pain of it howls like the April wind
Where I've been pushed against the rocks and there I'm pinned

I used to pay the bills with my amazing motor skills
I feared no challenge or endeavor
I just pushed for the ocean, come whatever

It was my favorite place on Earth, the place of my rebirth
This job was my life, not just my livin'
And I remember rowdy nights, and boatman fights
But the next day all was forgiven

But, now the adventures and the days
Are just kind of a haze
And all the faces have run together

I'm still just a poor man, those days are my only treasure
Down where the wind and rain, the solace and pain
Mix with the rum and the whiskey and run together

Oh, I should have known better
No, I never should have left her

But the river's pull was strong, and the season was long
And I returned to find that she'd moved on

It was as simple as missing a stroke in Hance
You just don't get another chance

Oh, I saw the face of Wonder Itself, a truly generous gift
But believe me Baby, that wasn't the veil I wanted to lift

And I still stare at the stars, and wonder where you are
And think about the life that could have been ours
I think it's something that I'll regret forever

I know it was wrong to keep her waiting
But now my memories of her are fading
They've mixed with the rum and the whiskey
And run together

I'd like to run that old river one more time
Just to feel again how young I used to feel
Back when I was confident and brave, and nobody's slave
With the strength of a bull, and nerves of steel

If it's something I'm gonna do
I'm gonna run with my old crew
They may cuss and fight, and spit and lie
But the life they live is true

So how 'bout it Debo, Zimmer, Butch and Heather
Meet me at the Ferry and one more time we'll run together

C'mon Wolfie Man, Brecky Boy, Bret, Carrie, whoever
Meet me at the Ferry and one last time let's run together

An Autumn Walk

I descend into the canyon through a vein
of gold-leafed aspens and red-leafed oaks.
The trees look like a parade of hekatonkheires
each arm carrying a lit manora.

Walking through the trees, lit with the soft,
careful Autumn light is like walking through a
garden of chandeliers.

All about me leaves detach and fall. For
foxes, deer and poets a ticker tape parade.
The leaves come in every color of the Autumn
harvest: the bright yellow of squash, the soft
yellow of pears, the orange of pumpkins, the
red-brown of russet potatoes, and the flame
of the deer hunter's campfire.

I follow a trail that follows a stream into the
interior of the forest. The trail covered with
fallen leaves. The edges of the fallen leaves,
with veins like a gin-drinker's nose, are
stenciled in frost.

The stream I follow comes to a still pool. I detach my backpack and kneel at its edge to drink. The still water reflects the red and gold leaves of the trees. Like drinking from a stained-glass window.

Dancing Around a Desert Campfire

I pitched my tent without thought of where the door
Should be facing; I pitched it where I did, facing it how I
Did because it was the only flat spot, the only bare
Spot among the junipers, beavertail, millet grass, and
Ledges, corduroyed with lichen.

Later I followed some deer tracks across the sand to a
Small basin of water and I knelt and filled my canteen.
Later still I built a campfire and warmed my can of stew,
Ate it while warming my back against the fire.

And as darkness became complete I took a brand from
The fire and again turned to the darkness and waved it
About creating streaks and tracers. I drew stars, Maurer
Roses, and frivolous calligraphy in the air, that appeared
And vanished as quickly as these sweet, solitary days in
The beautiful desert.

While drawing something new across the desert sky with
My brand I heard the plaintive howl of the coyote. My hand
Paused. Electric tickles surged up my spine like I'd put my hand
On a Van de Graaff generator. I leapt upon the cliff ledge and
Howled back. About thirty seconds

Later a Gibbous moon rose over the cliff wall.
Yeah, we did that!

I know from past experience that after three evenings of
Standing and dancing around a desert campfire that my
Clothes will absorb that great campfire smell that will
Linger on in their fibers for weeks to come. My hope is

That as my clothes have absorbed that great campfire
Smell, so let the experience of these four short days in
The desert be absorbed into my body, my consciousness
My soul, and remain there for weeks to come. And may
The beauty of these days become me.
Like the milk of the milkweed, in its own way, becomes
The butterfly.

A Backpacker's Rain Delay

Rumble of kettle drums [offstage right] indicates that
the storm is still four Mississippis away.

I make my way across the canyon floor
and pick out a cliff ledge
to serve as my balcony. I feel like a Count
with my poncho billowing out dramatically behind me.
I take my seat among a well-dressed sorority of junipers. Below,
in the cheap seats, the tall
autumn grasses continue their pre-curtain susurrus.

THE SETTING:
The interior of Spring Gulch. An east-west running
canyon in southern Utah.

THE SCENE:
A sky painted to resemble a thick gray turkey
gravy. Pinatas, made to look like cumulonimbus dumplings, hang
from the ceiling. An umbrella skeleton to represent a windblown
spiderweb. Nose-against-screen door smell of oncoming rain.

The houselights dim. The cricket orchestra plays
their violins.

[Enter thunder and lightning, stage right].

The clouds bare their lightning fangs,
an X-ray of a winterbare cottonwood,
held upside down. Thunder crumbles through the
canyon, pinballing cliff to cliff to cliff with a sound of Navajo
warriors grinding skulls with a mano and metate.
Or   Croutons crushed with rolling pin.

The ghosts of the ancient warriors rise to strike
the cloud piñatas with their staves.

[Enter female rain]
Which patters on the rocks and sand like polite golf applause.

The female rain is soft and warm. Played by Mom's Hug,
Airport Kisses, Thanksgiving Day Nap, Vacation Snapshot,
Bedtime Stories, Letter from Home.
The storm intensifies.

[Exit female rain, stage left. Enter male rain, stage right]
The male rain is played by Tridents, Pitchforks, Bayonets,
Vengeful Hornets, Two-Year-Old Tantrums,
Kamikaze Arrows

At the climax of the play the lightning elbows
each other out of the way, the thunder so dense
it steps on the lines of the one before it.

Lightning flashes hang from the clouds
like the phosphorescent tentacles of a jellyfish.
Or   At other times, sleek and narrow
as the crack in the Liberty Bell.

Thunder may come in hitches, that of sobs catching in the throat
Or   A pith helmet tumbling down stairs.

The Rain moves to center stage. And just stands there
legs together, back straight. As if he's about to deliver the play's
great monologue.
But he says nothing. Just stands there. Just to let me feel his
mighty presence. Infuse me with awe,
meekness, fear, reverence.

The power that directs the winds. That decides upon
drought, flood, life. He laughs at dams.
It is he who fed the Anasazi, then shepherded them away when he
left. He was there when the Navajo emerged from their underworld
reed and saw him, and named him.

Another flare of lightning. X-ray of winterbare
cottonwood is illuminated again
this time at the back of stage right, half-hidden
behind the cliffwall. The thunder sounds like a
sheet ripping in Morse Code: dot-dot-daaash.
Or   Seven couch pillows fired from seven muskets.

At last the female rain and the male rain unite under the
costumes of Chinese dragons. And leap
from every clifftop
Stage right, stage center, stage left.

[Exit Rain] As he leaves he sweeps the canyon floor clean.
In a flash, with a flood.

Shaft of lemon-water sunlight falls center stage, falling upon
sunflowers, their windblown petals gathered around their heads
like sunbonnets. Heads bowed as they humbly receive

My one man standing ovation.

It's Enough I Get to Watch

I'd like to hold the desert star in my hand
When it opens its petals. I'd like to be the blossom
That fuels the busy hummingbird.

I'd like to be the tree on which the buck rubs his itchy
Green antlers to scrape off the velvet. I'd like to be the
Stream along which the elegant Cottonwoods grow.

I'd like to be the mud bank that the river otters slide
Down in their hour of play. I want to be the morning's
First rays that inspires the choir of birds in the aspens.
I want to be the song the mockingbird sings.

But it is enough that I get to be

The man who wanders the splendid woods and watches
It happen.

The Chapel of Shadows and Sunbeams

The last of the day's sunlight
Enters at a slant.
The canyon's rough skin
A vitiligo of shadows and light.

Silence is the explorer's favorite sermon,
And my reason for coming here is to hear it again.

The curves and turns in the canyon become
Sharper here, morphing from the Blackjack
Table's gentle curve to the more aggressive turn
Of the hairpin.

Up there, at times, it seems that
God
Has been replaced by
god
Of the lower case. Or worse, an Homunculus.
But here I can still feel that which is capital in God.

Or maybe it's just the motes in my eye
Or the beams—and I have a few—
Prevent me from seeing what they're seeing.

The cliff walls, which were strictly vertical, are now
Severely undercut so that their rims
Lean out over their bases a good 40 feet, like the
Open lids on grand pianos.

Here in this chapel of shadows and sunbeams
There is no need to wait for the rapture.
And how many miracles have I beheld?

My offering, forgive me Lord, is smaller than
Even the Widow's Mite. I've little to offer
Beyond a prayer of thanks, but I gladly give it
At the end of each beautiful day.

I cross the humble stream one more time and
Come to my evening's campsite, a bench of packed
Sand on the inside curve of the stream, below Jacob
Hamblin Arch.

Down here my soul sings
Without any prompting from a chorister.
Earlier today I pushed through a heavy patch of
Willows and reeds, grunting and cussing, but emerged
Into the clear, covered with dozens of ladybugs.
I mean, how could my soul not sing?

I have found my joy, my revelation,
My sanctuary, and at last my peace
Here, in my wild desert chapel
I confess.

I Am a Poet

"How can you even call yourself that"
She says, "You've published
Next to nothing."
But a plum tree is still a plum tree.

And a magnolia is still a magnolia.
A primrose is still a primrose.
And a lupine is still a lupine.
Though they may take a while to bloom.

An Orangeville Apple

Like me it spent the summer soaking up the sun.
I drank the same water that it drank.
I too took nourishment from this soil.
I too was bruised by hailstorms.
Like it, a caring person noticed me before I fell.

I hold a box of Orangeville apples under my arm
As I kiss my mom and dad goodbye
To take back to my hermit's apartment.

And as I pull out of the driveway I take my first
Bite. I once again taste the rain, those beautiful
Sun-soaked days and the soil I once plowed and
Dug into.

You, apple, like me, won't put down roots until
First you've been chewed up and spit out.

I honk as I pull out and mom and dad wave goodbye
From the porch. You apple, like me, will not have
Roots, but it's good to have parents that do.

An Elegy for my Old Hiking Boots

Do you remember how high we jumped that
time we mistook the dry leaf scratching across
the slickrock for a rattlesnake's warning? Or
the time Escalante River quicksand tried to
vacuum you off my feet?

We've left tracks in some great places my old
friends. In the San Rafael Swell, in Grand
Gulch, Arches, Antelope Canyon, the Lamar
Valley.

And now you grow ragged, your soles have
grown holey. The time has come to set you
aside. But it simply wouldn't do to bury you
in a landfill smothered by the very trash you
so joyfully carried me away from.

Should I close you back up in the box you
came in and bury you, complete with head-
stone and epitaph? Or would you rather be
cremated and sprinkled over your favorite
places to once again commune with the dust
of southern Utah, Arizona, Yellowstone,
British Columbia? No, I have a better idea.

I know a place where I can take you. It's a
place where the crickets fiddle long into the
night, that place where ravens sit in the wind-
twisted junipers. Where the sky is narrow
between canyon walls. We've been there
before.

You are so light in my hand as I pick you up.
You are freckled with blue raft paint, pocked
from wayward campfire sparks. Your toes are
grass-stained, and tipped upward as if picking
up the scent of a new trail. You are frayed,
coming unglued. Your souls so thin. You slip
on so easily. You fit me so well.

I'm going to miss you old friends. You
watched from the bank as I swam in
Yellowstone's Boiling River. You have stood
next to the tent flap like two puppies eager
to be let out.

We have crept up on elk, butterflies, daisies,
Anasazi ruins. Deer, wild turkeys and squirrels
ran from us the time we ran through the woods
so exuberant and free.

You romped on the gas pedal with such lust
as we careened out of town. I have wrapped a
shirt around you and used you for a pillow and
tucked my glasses inside the other for
safekeeping.

I have seen you turn chalky white after the sea
salt evaporated off you. I have heard your
hollow thump against British Columbia's
spongy forest floors.

If your tongues could talk you would tell
of the times you carried me through
Yellowstone snow, Arizona mud, Uinta
frost, over Zion slickrock.

Many times I have leaned back against a log
or a rock with my legs splayed out before me
and watched the sun set between you, my
sunset gunsight.

How many miles have we seen together? How
many sunrises. How many hills have we
climbed? But they were too few, too few.
I now feel every stone and stick through your
thin soles. I feel the heat emanating from the
sandstone. How short the last trail is.

I have seen the world with the help of your
many eyes. I have tasted the marrow of
life through your tongues.

Someday, I hope many years from now, when
my soul is ready to cast off its old body, I
hope it asks my body—as I now ask you my
dear hiking boots—"Do you have one more
trail left in you, old friend?" And when we walk
down the last trail I hope I feel every stone on
it, feel the heat of the sun coursing
into me. I hope when that time comes I am
covered in grass-stains, my cheeks wrinkled
from many days spent in the good sun. I hope
each of my scars tells an interesting story.

And when my soul finally slips off the old
body I hope that it does so with the same joy,
melancholy, reluctance, sadness, delight,
homesickness, wistfulness that I feel now for
you my eager, dutiful, reliable hiking boots.

When we reach the end of the trail I will face
you toward the west, beneath the crooked
junipers I love so much. Down amongst the
Brigham tea and prickly pears. Overlooking
this tributary of the Escalante. Here you will
still have sand beneath you, here beloved dust
shall cover you again.

But first we will dance around the campfire
one last time as I engrave your epitaph into
the night with an ember-tipped stick.

A New Story

The river that day was thick and gray
From a recent influx of Paria clay
It mirrored the sky of an overcast day
The river was calm as a windless bay

We're done with Hance, a hard row to hoe
We made it through Crystal a hard one to row
And Horn Creek tried to crack us
But we've had too much practice
But Lava Falls, oh boy!, still lies down below

Yeah, give me a thousand days like these
One of a long row of boatmen floating at ease
Drifting on flatwater, our oars tucked beneath our knees
Enjoying the clouds, and a rare August breeze

A canyon wren calls from the acacia trees
Complementing the river's soliloquies
Bighorns are grazing on the river banks
And the ravens are up to their usual pranks

We still have twenty miles left to go
So under feigned protest I let my passenger row
I lie back on the frame and take in the show
And admire the view that's above my toes

Our sky may be narrow but our world is wide
Just half a skoshe smaller than a boatman's pride
"Just keep to the grease and let `er glide"
I tell my passenger in a whispered aside

On and on the river wends, and the canyon bends
I'm filled with a homesick feeling as another season ends
Because few things are better: Hallelujah! Amen!
Than exploring this heaven with my wild friends

Oh, I love being a river guide
I get to work and play all day outside

Outside the lines, outside the box
Outside Society's pestilent pox

Outside the swarm, outside the norm
Outside the annoying need to conform

Outside your wifi signals and cell phone range
`Cause I'm analog baby, I know, it's strange
We love it down here, where nobody owns us
There's no one to impress, not even the Joneses

Sure, we aint got no insurance, or IRA
We aint got no benefits or 401(k)

Down here we traded our Mondays
And home-improvement Saturdays
For sunnier, funnier, adrenalized gladder days

'Cause, I've sacrificed too many of my big dreams
On that sneaky altar of Some Day
But not this one. Not this place. Not this feeling.
Not this time
This time it's different! This is the Big Fish
The One that aint gonna get away

It was a hard life full of sweat and grit
But all hardships aside, still hard to admit
It was time to say goodbye
Though my life here on the river was rich
I somehow got that movin'-on itch
Though the question wasn't so much a "when?"
        as a "why?"

To stay or to go, it's hard making future plans
When there's a breeze at your back and oars in your hands

I know of a paradise in the middle of nowhere
And if ya wanna get there ya gotta row there
The light and cliff walls put on quite a show there
So pack the raft babe, it's time to go there

I have a shelf back home crowded with knickknacks
A fond river memory attached to each one
There's driftwood and polished rocks
A Weebie stick, and a broken oar
There's a mangled prop, a rubber duck
And lots, lots more

It tells a long twisting story of this daring adventure
With exploration and this river at its epicenter

Now . . . let's fast forward, to season eight
Life was good, everything going great

I was drinking Blue Moon in my favorite bar
Telling a story about my favorite scar

I'd just reached the crux of my narration
Where the plot expanded under poetic aeration

My eyes took on a mischievous glint
As I dropped, foreshadow-like, a devious hint

Then I spun around on my stool and there she was
My head started reeling, my heart set abuzz

I lost all thought when we locked eyes
They were the blueish gray of northern skies

I saw deep in her eyes, and I saw true
I saw something old, something new
Something borrowed, something blue
And that, my friends, was how I knew

"Hi!' she said. "I'm Dana" (the swamper's sister)
I was already picturing all the places I'd kiss her

"I'm coming with you (*forever!*)
Tomorrow on your river trip."
Oh, such beautiful news!
And falling from such beautiful lips!

She wore a red tank top and a tight black skirt
I just sat there frozen, too flustered to flirt

I managed to mumble, "Hello, I'm Steve."
Then I shook her hand and took my leave

Every long-term boatman has been thrown from the raft
Yeah it happens, even though I'm a master of my craft

And I've been held underwater till I was out of air
It felt just like that when I saw her brushing her hair

And during my river days I've had butterflies aplenty
Above Crystal, Lava Falls and Hance
But the butterflies this time were different
When she reached over and held my hand

She's the line I hang on to when the raft goes over
She's my campfire at the end of the trail
She's the context that makes my lifeline make sense
She's the universe packed in a shotgun shell

She's the heartbeat that drums my worries to sleep
She's the tea leaves at the bottom of the Nomad's Grail
She's the stake inside the heartache
She's as beautiful as Venus as she stepped from her shell

Before the trip was over we started making plans
And those butterflies again, just like dropping into Hance

Ours was the pain of the journey at parting
Entwined with the joy of a new one just starting

We stood by the river and said our goodbyes
With my beloved river reflected in her eyes

It made my goodbye twice as hard to say
'Cause I also said goodbye to the river that day

Yeah, it's a strange deal, it's kinda surreal
When you see your endless summer coming to an end
It's hard to say goodbye to the river
When that river's been your savior and your best friend

The world had beat me up, and broke me
And that river was my balm, my bandage and my suture
The river was my map, my true love, my everything . . .
My everything but the future

My heart just screams when I think of those Big Dreams
That I sacrificed on the altar of "Some Day,"
But not today. Not this time. Not her, for she's The One
She's 'The One' I won't let get away

'Cause I know of a house in the middle of a city
It's simple, yet charming, cozy and pretty
It's home to a happy dog and a curious kitty
And the beautiful woman who built it with me

Yet here I sit by this river, and man, I still love it
I want to keep it, guard it, hold it and hug it
I cherish it, I want it, I desperately need it
I drink it, I sweat it, I literally bleed it

It's my refuge, my chapel, my holy water
It's my teacher, my life lab, my alma mater
It was my launchpad after that long-ago crash
It's the place where I rose like a phoenix from the ash

But . . . there's a wall back home with a long empty shelf
That we plan to fill with our lives' worth of knickknacks
With a beautiful memory attached to each one
And it will create a door, a most wondrous door
That will somehow reach to eternity and back

That shelf will hold all our many magical moments
Our life story told through symbol and allegory
And it will tell the tale of the greatest adventure of all . . .
And it will be a love story!

Heater Smell

I walk out my front door today
To look, to touch, to encounter
To find
A comfortably chilly morning. Cold
Enough that the sandy trail I soon join
Glitters with frost. Just cold enough for a
Thin sweater.

I walk past kids selecting pumpkins for
Jack-o-lanterns. Past sharp-scented willows
And onto a plateau where I watch the early
Morning sun spread across the buttes, towers
Cliffs and dunes.

Today, over the Midwestern plains the brave
Geese skim the trees and press on to lakes
And ponds of the south. In Yellowstone the
Black Bears and Grizzlies have noticed the
Shortening of days and are having thoughts of
Hibernation. In Orangeville, beautiful Orangeville,
The leaves of the glorious Cottonwoods are turning yellow.

When after my curiosity has been sated
And my soul coerced back into a shape I
Better prefer I return home –though I'm not
Sure *home* is the right word for this rented room
Where I keep a bed during the river season—

I navigate through cardboard boxes which are
Packed, stacked, taped shut and turn on the heater
For the first time since April and smell
The dust burning off the element. It's a smell
I have grown to love, more so for the associat-
Ions I ascribe to it. After eight seasons of river
Running the smell of burning dust now signals
The end of the season and time to be moving on.
Only this year, when I move on, I will finally be
Coming home, *at last!*

To her.

Coming Home

The best part about the desert is feeling its emptiness
The best part about a tent is its huge backyard
The best part about a campfire is the way it illuminates
    the universe
The best part about a backpack is the way it gently pushes me
    in the direction of my dreams
The best part of the compass is the tingle it gives me in my spine
The best part of the map is its white spaces
The best part about walking is letting my imagination run ahead
The best part about walking up the home path is her silhouette
    in the window

A Prayer of Thanks

A spontaneous prayer leaps from my heart as
I start down the morning trail. Perhaps it jumps
Through the door left open when Joy leapt from
My heart, as I hoisted the pack on my back and
Started down a trail, never before explored. By me.

Thank you, He who created the morning glory that
Twines up the Cottonwood tree, with its tiny pink
And white flowers, which create bright constellations
In the darkened spaces of the woods.

Thank you that I, once again, have a pack on my back
And an unexplored trail beneath my feet. Thank you
For blessing me with strong legs and good health.
Thank you for the eyes to see the beauty You have
Created, the cognition to process it.

And I think some measure of courage is needed to
Walk into an unfamiliar, wild place alone. Thanks, too,
For that. Thank you for my ears which, even now,
Hear the wild turkeys, clucking and bellowing. Cooing,
Contentedly—it sounds—as they scratch in the
Damp leaves.

Thank you, He who made the wild, untrammeled places.
Thank you for the flowering prickly pears, with yellow lint in
their belly buttons. And farther down the trail I encounter a
group of cone-throated flowers gathered among the dried grasses
like a red-gowned choir, their faces uplifted skyward joining
me in singing the day's Hallelujahs. And I can't even believe the
butterflies! So splendid and
Perfect.

Thank you for blessing me
With an explorer's curious mind, and a poet's appreciative,
thankful heart which is tuned to the delicate resonance given off
by the natural world
Which I count as my two greatest gifts.

Thank you for this beautiful canyon, today's perfect weather,
and a day free of duty that I might explore it.

And Lord, there is a good woman who waits for me
To return. She has a gentle, patient way. Thank you for the long,
winding trail (You know how much I love those!) that led me
to her.

I Get Close

From a far-flung corner of the globe
I'm at last on that blessed homeward road

I roll up the maps, and strap on my pack
I've seen enough—for now—I'm going back

Back to the blue slate hills, and the waving wheat fields
That I, as a younger man, a hundred times tilled

But they were sown with the tares of restlessness
That grew to an age of recklessness

I heard the road singing its siren song
And any freedom song was my anthem
In my pocket were the seeds of adventure
And I wandered the world in a quest to plant them

And I've been down more than a thousand trails
In my quest to find the Nomad's Grail

It's just beyond the next horizon
It's just past the next bend
For the quest for the Nomad's Grail
Is a quest without end

Yet now I can't stop picturing how great it will be
Sharing the old stories at the table with my family

Where my mom, dad, grandma and grandpa
Watch over our own little Shangri-La

It is a young man's nature to ramble and roam
And lucky is the man whose compass points home

If life is an apple, love is the tree
And home is the soil in which it grows
If life is a raft, love is the river
And home is the mountain from which it flows

Home is our island, home is our highland
Home is the bird with the sprig in its beak
If life is a book, she's my favorite story
And love is the language that we speak

If life is a kite, love is the wind
And home is the bond that lets it fly
If life is a song, love is the choir
And home is the stage where it amplifies

There's no pull so strong as the homeward tug
And there's nothing as warm as a homecoming hug

Home is the kingdom that crowned us
Home is the roots that ground us
Only the walls of a Home
Can contain a love that is boundless

There's only one place I can hear my favorite words
Words more beautiful than any poem
They're spoken by the sweetest voice I've ever heard
It's the joyful sound of "Welcome Home!"

Now I walk through the blowing dust in the heat of noon
Then through the falling dew in the cool of the moon

And now, after all those miles, and the traveler's trials
After so many lost and lonely roads
After all the loss and gain, the triumph and the pain
I'm finally getting close

I get close to the Castle Gate
And those old familiar places
I get close to the alkali flats
And those beautiful sunburnt mesas

I get close to the place where you said the words
    I already knew
I get close to the girl who made my greatest dream
    come true

I get close to that spot where you said, "Yes!"
I can picture you there, shining! in your summer dress

I get close, and my heart makes that familiar sound
Of wild horses running on open ground

Baby, I don't know if I'll make it home tonight
But keep the porch light on, 'cause I just might

I've been gone too long and I apologize
But I do have an excuse
But it has as many holes
As the soles of these old shoes

They're covered with a crust of old road dust
And they've been washed in ocean foam
They're roughly used, but they're a good pair of shoes
For they know a shortcut home

Now, my old house didn't look like much
What it really needed was a woman's touch

It had a sturdy roof that held out the storms
And a cozy fireplace that kept me warm

It had a table made of common planks
Where I ate my bread and gave my thanks

It had a bed, but it was missing the girl of my dreams
I'd wonder where she was as I stared up at the beams

It had a window that looked out on this beautiful world
All that was missing was the beautiful girl

It had a door that kept my troubles at bay
And opened to reveal tomorrow's adventure
And then one beautiful, magical day
Through that door my true love entered

Home is the kingdom that crowned us
Home is the roots that ground us
Only the walls of a Home
Can contain a love that is boundless

There's only one place I can hear my favorite words
Words more beautiful than any poem
They're spoken by the sweetest voice I've ever heard
It's the joyful sound of "Welcome Home!"

Printed in the United States
By Bookmasters